let's travel in

CANADA

Edited by Joan Downing and Frances Dyra

CENTRAL MISSOURI
STATE COLLEGE
Warrensburg

WITHDRAWN BY
JAMES C. KIRKPATRICK LIBRARY
TECHNICAL SERVICES

A TRAVEL PRESS BOOK

D1072347

JE
917.1
D75

PICTURE ACKNOWLEDGMENTS

The full-color pictures and illustrations in this book are the work of the following photographers and artists, whose collaboration is gratefully acknowledged.

Ralph R. Brooks (pages 23, 32, 43, 47, 55, 67); National Film Board of Canada (pages 17, 19, 20, 24, 28, 31, 35, 36, 39, 40, 44, 48, 52, 56, 64, 68, 72, 75, 79); Canadian Government Travel Bureau (pages 27, 59, 71); Ontario Department of Tourism and Information (page 51); Manitoba Department of Industry and Commerce, Winnipeg (pages 60, 63); Yukon Department of Travel (page 76).

For the black-and-white photographs we wish to thank Ralph R. Brooks (pages 8, 26, 42, 49, 65); National Film Board of Canada (pages 10, 22, 37, 38, 50, 53, 54, 69, 77); Alberta Government Travel Bureau (page 13); Canadian Government Travel Bureau (pages 45 and 66); Montreal Travel Bureau (page 30); Wide World Photos (page 41); Manitoba Department of Industry and Commerce, Winnipeg (page 61). The map was made by Robert Borja.

Library of Congress Catalog Card No. 68-14729
Copyright © 1968 by Regensteiner Publishing Enterprises, Inc.
All rights reserved. Printed in the U.S.A. Published simultaneously in Canada.

CONTENTS

265213

U.S.

Yukon

31

26

Northwest Territories

British Columbia

20

Alberta

EDMONTON

VICTORIA

28

25

17

PACIFIC OCEAN

19

REGINA

Saskatchewan

Churchill River

29

Hudson

Manitoba

30

23

WINNIPEG

24

22

United States

Locales of thirty-two full-page pictures

CANADA, A VAST AND VARIED LAND

CANADA is a vast land, occupying more than half of the North American continent. It is a land of sweeping panoramas from the Atlantic to the Pacific and from the cold wastes of Hudson Bay to the bustle and commerce of the Great Lakes basin and the long sea arm of the St. Lawrence Seaway.

It is the second-largest country in the world and has great natural wealth, beauty, and grandeur. Canada's progress of the past and potential for the future are recognized throughout the world. The country has found its pride in the busy cities of the East and the natural wealth and beauty of the central plains and western mountains.

As we travel through Canada, we will discover many surprises in this huge country. In the North, we see Eskimos hunting and fishing in the Arctic Tundra, where it is so cold that trees cannot grow. In the eastern provinces, fishing boats dart between giant ocean steamers. The province of Quebec greets us with a charm entirely its own—both French and English, quaint and exciting, where the cities of Montreal and Quebec are historical showplaces. In the province of Ontario, we will see the bustling activities of business, industry, and government in Ottawa and Toronto. Field after field of wheat whispering in the sun will lead us to the West, where there are cowboys and Indians, beautiful lakes for fishing, mountains to climb, and forests for lumbering. Beyond the splendor of the Rockies, miles of giant trees thrive in the moist coastal climate and salmon boats gleam in the Pacific.

Canada is a surprise because she contains these varied faces. Truly, this is a country with something to offer everyone.

BRITISH AND FRENCH INFLUENCE

As in the rest of the western hemisphere, Indians were the original inhabitants of Canada. It is believed that they came to this land about 10,000 years ago, crossing the Bering Strait from Asia to America. The Eskimos are thought to have followed the same route 5000 years later.

An Englishman, John Cabot, first reached the shores of what is now Canada in 1497 when he discovered Newfoundland. It was a Frenchman, however, Jacques Cartier, who took possession of the land in 1534 in the name of the French king. Fishermen, fur traders, and missionaries emigrated to the new land in great numbers, but there was no organized colonization until 1604. In that year, Samuel de Champlain, sent to manage the fur trade, founded the first permanent French colony at Port Royal, now Annapolis, Nova Scotia. Four years later, he began the settlement of Quebec.

This was an era of frequent skirmishes between Great Britain and France, and control of the area moved back and forth between the two countries. Eventually, Britain's superior command of the seas enabled her to capture Quebec in 1759. A year later, the French army in Canada surrendered. By the treaty called the Peace of Paris, Canada was formally given to Great Britain in 1763.

Since that time, Canada has remained British. American Revolutionaries unsuccessfully attacked Quebec in 1776, hoping to spread their new ideas over the entire continent. Later, Canada became a refuge and home for tens of thousands of American Loyalists who sided with the British.

Most notable of Canada's brave frontiersmen was Alexander Mackenzie, a fur trapper, who was the first man to travel across the country by land. Mackenzie reached the Pacific in 1793.

In the rough frontier towns, the Northwest Mounted Police, predecessors of today's Royal Canadian Mounted Police, began the efficient keeping of law and order that is proudly continued today.

Fort Prince of Wales in Manitoba was one of the British defense posts against the French.

On July 1, 1867, Canada became the first federal union in the British Empire. In 1926, Canada and the other British dominions were declared to be partner nations with Britain, equal in status, and bound together only by an allegiance to a common crown.

NATION OF CONTRASTS

Canada is cut in two by the Canadian Shield, a huge rocky area covering over two-thirds of the country. The Shield is one of the oldest volcanic rock formations in the world. Shield country is barren except for a few partly fertile areas. The melting of the glaciers in the Ice Age removed most of the land's soil.

Geographically and economically, Canada can be divided into five areas:

THE ATLANTIC COAST—DEPENDENCY ON THE OCEAN

The people of Newfoundland, New Brunswick, Nova Scotia, and Prince Edward Island derive both their living and their pleasure from the Atlantic Ocean. Quiet coves, rivers, and streams contrast sharply with busy shipping ports that carry Canada's products across the world.

Fishing is important industrially to all these provinces. Other products, however, are also important. In Nova Scotia, "The Fisherman's Haven," the lumber industry outranks fishing as one of the province's main sources of income. More than three-fourths of New Brunswick is forested, and its pulp and paper mills provide the chief sources of income. The port at Saint John is free of ice throughout the year. Along with Halifax, Nova Scotia, it is one of Canada's most important winter ports. The province of Newfoundland, which is made up of the island of Newfoundland and the coast of Labrador, produces great quantities of newsprint. In Canada's smallest province, the crescent-shaped Prince Edward Island, agriculture is the chief source of income, with both cattle and dairy products thriving abundantly in the damp climate.

ONTARIO AND QUEBEC—BUSY PROVINCES

Served by the St. Lawrence Seaway and the Great Lakes, Quebec and Ontario represent the industrial wealth of Canada.

Ontario is the leading manufacturing province, responsible for about forty per cent of Canada's income and half of all her manufactured goods. It is also the chief mineral-producing province. Ontario, like most of Canada, is highly dependent on water transport. Toronto, the provincial capital, is Canada's second-largest city and focal point of the nation's railways and businesses. Ottawa is the national capital.

Quebec is Canada's largest province. The virtually unexplored North is rich in ores, particularly copper and gold. Montreal is the hub of financial and industrial concerns and Canada's largest port. The provincial capital, Quebec City, is also a shipping and manufacturing center. After manufacturing, forests and farmlands are Quebec's most important assets. Quebec is the most urbanized of all the provinces, but there are still large numbers of small family farms.

MONTREAL—A FRENCH DESSERT

Montreal, built on an anvil-shaped island at the mouth of the St. Lawrence Seaway, is perhaps the most exciting city in Canada. Three-quarters of the city's population is French-speaking. Street signs, advertisements, and shopwindows reflect the city's mixed heritage. Even over the wild hysteria of a hockey crowd, the voice of the announcer gives information on the winning goal in both French and English.

Today Canada's largest city with a population of over 2,000,000, Montreal began as an Indian village called "Hochelaga." The origin of the name Montreal is uncertain. Some say it was named in honor of Cardinal de Medici, archbishop of Montreale, Sicily; others say it was named for a nobleman on Cartier's ship, who was lord of an estate in France known as "Montreal." The little village soon became the headquarters of the fur trade in the New World.

To know Montreal, it is said, is to know Canada. She is French and English, old and new, fun-loving and humming with industry. She is the headquarters of gourmet eating and nightlife, but she is also America's largest inland seaport and the center of Canada's cultural achievements. She is as old as Château de Ramezay and the seamen's church, Notre Dame de Bonsecours, and as new as the shining towers and underground shopping plaza of Plece. Montreal is a gracious hostess to more than two million tourists a year, who come to see plays and opera in the Place des Arts, eat in French restaurants, and tour the nightclub areas. The tourists also find a bookful of history and one of the world's most modern cities.

THE PRAIRIES—A RICH LAND

The Prairie Provinces of Manitoba, Saskatchewan, and Alberta are rich areas of flat plains bordered by mountains, lakes, and forests. Throughout these provinces, agriculture is important. Saskatchewan alone supplies more than half of Canada's total wheat output.

Manitoba, the easternmost of the Prairie Provinces, is becoming more and more dependent on manufacturing as its main source of income. Her capital, Winnipeg, is an important transportation center. Manitoba has a saltwater port at Churchill on Hudson Bay.

Alberta, to the west, possesses vast resources. Oil and natural gas are found in immense quantities, although wheat farming and cattle are still vital sources of income. The most diversified of the Prairie Provinces, Alberta is a mixture of modern towns and cities and untapped natural treasures. Especially in its northern Peace River district, where the wheat grows tall and fast under the midnight sun, Alberta is still a frontier.

CALGARY—REMNANT OF THE WILD WEST

Nearly every town in Alberta puts on a rodeo or stampede, but the biggest one of all takes place each summer in Calgary. Cowboys and ranchers from Canada and the United States participate in such events as bareback bronco riding, calf roping, and Brahma bull riding.

Steer decorating is one of the most colorful events of the Calgary Stampede. Following a custom begun in the old West by ranchers seeking to identify those cattle scheduled to go to market, cowboys race to place bright ribbons around a steer's horns.

A modern industrial oil town, Calgary goes thoroughly western for weeks before the Stampede. Chuckwagons, set up by stores whose employees take turns serving flapjacks, invade the streets. Nearly everyone wears ten-gallon white Stetson hats, cowboy boots, and western shirts. Businessmen arrive at their jobs dressed in western garb. At Stampede time, knowing how to ride a horse is unimportant— if you are in Calgary, you are a cowboy.

The Stampede itself begins with a huge parade led by the Royal Canadian Mounted Police and fully costumed Indians. Long into the night the sounds of the West can be heard through the windows of air-conditioned, modern hotels. It is easy to imagine that law enforcement is once again in the hands of a quick-drawing sheriff.

Calgary has many other attractions, including a park with life-size model dinosaurs, a marine museum, a zoo, and Heritage Park with its paddle-wheeler and old steam engine to ride in. Sixty miles away are the shining snow-capped Rockies.

Roping calves is a skill of the Old West still practiced today.

BRITISH COLUMBIA—BEAUTY ON THE PACIFIC

Isolated from the rest of Canada by the Rocky Mountains, British Columbia stretches along the coast of the Pacific Ocean. Lumber is the most important industry of this province; the most important trees are the Douglas fir and hemlock found on Vancouver Island. The valuable Pacific Sockeye Salmon has made fishing extremely successful. Unlike the Atlantic Provinces, fishing in British Columbia is a consistently profitable industry. The northernmost coast is reminiscent of

Scandinavia—forest-covered mountains crowding to the sea and the long fjord-like inlets, appearing suddenly here and there. The city of Vancouver is a busy port, a metropolis with half the province's population. It is almost surrounded by mountains.

THE NORTHWEST TERRITORIES AND THE YUKON— FLOWERS IN THE SNOW

Fascinating and still largely unexplored, the Yukon and Northwest Territories are frozen watchmen in Canada's North. This is grim country, where much of the land never thaws. It is a surprisingly rich country, containing metal, coal, and oil deposits which have been left dormant because of high development costs. Commercial fisheries have recently been begun by the government, and are proving quite successful. The northern three-fourths of the Territories lie in the Arctic zone, where shipping comes to a complete halt in October or November. Not until late July can ships move with safety.

Some think of the Northwest Territories as a huge outdoor scientific laboratory and a land of 100,000 lakes and streams. It is a place to mine for gold and other ores, a place where progress is conspicuous in the forms of radar domes, paved streets, and oil derricks. To the Eskimos, who total about one-third of the Territories' population, this land of ice is home.

There is a pioneering spirit throughout the land. In many small settlements, women run households skillfully despite the fact that food and other necessities can be ordered only once a year. Hardy grains and vegetable crops can be grown in the South, and in nearly every settlement, flower gardens brighten the bleakness of the land.

The Territories and the Yukon are governed in part by the federal government and in part by a territorial legislative body, which has some of the responsibilities of a Canadian provincial government.

ROOM TO GROW

There is space in Canada. Over ninety per cent of her people live in a two-hundred-mile-wide belt along the border of the United States, and even here there is room for millions more people.

There is a great Canadian potential, springing from this same spaciousness and the possibility of new ventures. Joined by her great seaway to all the nations of the world, Canada is important in the world structure. Rich in the gifts of nature, her future will be great.

As we travel through Canada, let us enjoy all she has to offer. But let us notice, too, the excitement in the air of things to come, things left to do. The promise of Canada is important to what she is today—busy, proud, confident. She is worthy of being understood.

let's travel in

ST. LAWRENCE SEAWAY: MAKING OF A SEACOAST

THE St. Lawrence Seaway, built cooperatively by Canada and the United States, was dedicated in 1959. In its creation, over 6600 miles of land in the two countries were converted into another "seacoast," deep in the heart of the continent. The river and seaway are now the connecting links between the Great Lakes basin and the Atlantic Ocean.

More than a billion dollars was spent in constructing the seaway's seven locks, dredging a channel, constructing protective dikes, digging canals, raising some bridges and building new ones, and constructing a power dam and two control dams. The cost also included moving several towns, railroads, and highways. Many families were relocated to make room for the 100-square-mile lake in the St. Lawrence River, for which 38,000 acres of land were inundated. An historic community-museum, Upper Canada Village, used many buildings from inundated towns for its re-creations of the past.

Money, detailed work, and heartbreak went into the building of the seaway. But today, from mid-April to early December, ocean going vessels dock at Chicago, Detroit, Montreal, Toronto, and other ports along the 1185-mile seaway system, bringing to the North American continent such diverse items as marble, apricots, glassware, candies, coffee, raw sugar, olives, and leather goods. To ports of the seven seas, they take grain, synthetic rubber, steel, cars, meat, refrigerators, logs, machinery, vitamins, soybeans, and hundreds of other products.

Men had talked of constructing a seaway since the early 1800's, in the heyday of canal building, and small ocean vessels have long been able to pass through the old canals. But dissent and disagreement on both sides of the border kept actual ground breaking for a big project from beginning until 1954. Today, with every ship that slowly makes its way through the seaway's locks, the future of the industries of Canada and the United States does indeed grow more rosy.

NEWFOUNDLAND FISHERMAN: A LIVING FROM THE WATERS

THE Newfoundlander's saying, "Fair weather to you and snow to your heels," is more than a wish of good luck. It is a prayer. Deep-sea fishing can be a sport for some, but as a livelihood, it is rugged and risky. This fisherman has spent his life gathering tuna, cod, and halibut from the waters of the Atlantic. Sometimes the waters are calm and sometimes they are not, but each day he must go out in his boat.

Off Newfoundland, the gray Atlantic waves roll over flat underwater ridges, or "banks." Fleets of trawlers from many nations come to the largest of these—the Grand Banks—to fish the rich waters.

Life is rough in Newfoundland. Simple wooden, fenced houses sprawl in the villages of this land of rolling hills, evergreen forests, and wilderness. It is a silent country. In Labrador, the mainland portion of the province, there are few roads through the tundra.

The visiting sports fishermen come to fish in the lakes and streams that make up almost one-third of the surface area of the province. Caribou, bear, and moose await the game hunter. To sports-loving visitors, this is a land of plenty. They are impressed by the capital, Saint John's, which had settlers as early as 1540 and is one of the oldest cities in North America. Vikings are believed to have landed here as early as 1000 A.D., and in the centuries that followed, the "new-found land" was visited by John Cabot and other early explorers.

To those who must live from the land, however, Newfoundland is a rocky and infertile country of great rough-hewn beauty, still vast and unexplored. It is growing with new industry. Pulp and paper mills have become highly profitable, and the frozen fish industry is creating an ever-growing market. Vast mining projects have begun in Labrador, which is loaded with mineral wealth. Yet, life continues to be by and from the sea. "Praise the weather when you're ashore," the fishermen say, knowing it does no good to do so once you are in your boat. For no matter what the weather may be, they must go to sea.

PRINCE EDWARD ISLAND: FLOATING FARMLAND

THE fairest that may possibly be seen," Jacques Cartier said of Prince Edward Island when he reached its shores in 1534. Covered with a rich red loam soil that makes it a prosperous, million-acre farm, the island still is fair.

Prince Edward Island is almost entirely well-cultivated farmland. Green rolling meadows cover this smallest of Canada's provinces; potatoes are the mainstay crop of the economy. The islanders also raise cattle and have developed silver-fox farms.

The shores are lined with sandy beaches against which washes the warmest salt water north of Florida, brought by the north-flowing Gulf Stream. From these waters, the islanders catch oysters and lobsters. Throughout the island, wild flowers grow in the mild climate. The streets of villages and towns are treelined, and well-kept flower gardens flourish in the fertile soil.

Charlottetown, the capital, is the birthplace of Confederation. Here the first meeting of the Fathers of Confederation was held in 1864, leading three years later to the Canadian Confederation. The new Confederation Center, which stands as a monument to that event, features a theater, art gallery, and museum. The room in which the Confederation meetings were held is nearby in the still-used provincial legislative buildings.

The island, despite its modern highways and towns, remains a sunny pastoral landscape, painted with the rich redness of the soil, the ever-changing greens of the land, and the sea-blue of the water dotted with white lighthouses. It is still very much the land described in *Anne of Green Gables*. Green Gables Farm attracts thousands of visitors every year.

LOUISBOURG
FORTRESS:
COMMAND
OF THE OCEAN

TWO centuries of French-English struggle for the rich Canadian wilderness are symbolized in the stones of Fort Louisbourg, high on a promontory overlooking the Atlantic Ocean. Located near what is now the port of Sydney, Nova Scotia, the fortress was built in 1717–20 of huge boulders cemented together. From it, the French defenders could easily see enemy ships four miles away.

The fort was one of New France's best strongholds against English attack, for the safeguarding of this walled city was necessary to retain control over the entire province. In 1758, however, the British attacked simultaneously with a naval fleet and land forces, and the fortress surrendered. Ten years later it was demolished. But even in its ruins, its strength could be seen. Now partially restored, the fort, and the area around it, is a National Historic Park.

The whole eastern seacoast of Canada is a continual echo of historic battles. Throughout the Maritime Provinces still stand round, stone forts called Martello towers. In the days of Napoleon, they were considered the best possible coastal fortress.

Shaded by trees, a Martello tower keeps watch over a now-peaceful land.

Above the city of Halifax is Battery Hill, site of the Citadel. This fort commands a clear view of Halifax Harbor. Now a National Historical Site, the Citadel today contains interesting museums as well as still-workable cannon.

Like silent watchmen, these seacoast forts and towers stand guard today over Canada's past.

NIAGARA FALLS:
BEAUTY AT WORK

ALL kinds of people come to Niagara Falls. As we stand by the railing, looking down on the clear, rushing water, we spot a bemused honeymoon couple with eyes only for each other, an engineer mentally calculating the kilowatt hours of power surging by, and a small boy whose eyes hold dreams of all the daredevils who have successfully gone over the falls in barrels, boxes, and other conveyances. Millions of people each year come to view the beauty, shared equally by Canada and the United States, of tons of sparkling water leaping hundreds of feet downward.

Probably the most famous tourist attraction in North America, the falls are something of a geological oddity. A hard layer of rock set on top of soft layers that have worn away has created the vertical drops known as the American Falls (167 feet) and Horseshoe Falls (at the top of the picture) on the Canadian side (158 feet). The wearing away of the under layer of rock is making the falls recede toward Lake Erie, and will eventually cause the drainage of that lake. (This is not expected to happen, however, for at least 25,000 years.) Horseshoe Falls has been receding at the rate of nearly five feet per year, and large chunks of the bank often break off. So the view we can see today will not be the same even a year from now.

For all of their majestic beauty, the falls are extremely useful. The peak summer force is 245,000 cubic feet per second, and about 130,000 cubic feet of water per second are diverted to electrical power, which Canada and the United States share equally. The falls can provide electricity for cities more than two hundred miles away, and are the major source of electrical power for the province of Ontario.

Wisely, both countries have recognized the rare beauty of the falls and take only a portion of the water to turn generators and light cities. The rest remains to awe and delight us.

NOVA SCOTIA: TREASURES IN THE OCEAN

FISHING the waters of the Atlantic has been a way of life in Nova Scotia ever since the Scots settled there in the 1700's. Nowhere in this Maritime Province are you more than thirty-five miles from the ocean. Gaily colored lobster floats, like the ones being painted here, bob like Christmas tree ornaments in the waters that teem with cod, haddock, scallops, and tuna. Even on land, "New Scotland" fishing serves as the province's main source of income with the packaging and processing of fish products a profitable and growing industry.

The waters off Nova Scotia are remarkable for more than their treasures of fish. Their surging force produces some of the highest tides in the world. Parrsboro Harbor is emptied completely every day by a tide that pulls the waters back more than a mile from the docks, leaving large, oceangoing ships sitting dry. In the Bay of Fundy, fishermen wait for the tide to go out, then drive wagons over the muddy ocean bottom to their nets to pull in their catch. Fundy's tides often form walls of water called "bores" more than forty feet tall, making this the greatest tide on earth.

Also in the Bay of Fundy is Isle Haute, known as "Treasure Island." Here, Edward Lowe, a pirate who cut off his victims' noses, is supposed to have buried his treasures more than two hundred years ago. The island has high tides and can be reached during only a few hours every day. Rocky cliffs 300 feet high surround it. In recent years, treasure hunters have found small amounts of gold and jewels, but stories say that hundreds of thousands of dollars in treasure still remain.

Peggy's Cove, on the southern coast of Nova Scotia, is a picturesque fishing village.

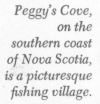

Although Nova Scotia's forested rocky soil can support little crop farming, dairy farming is important. The province looks to the sea, however, for its most valuable treasures.

NEW BRUNSWICK
FISHING WEIR

THINGS in New Brunswick have a tendency to do just the opposite of what you might expect. At the Reversing Falls on the Saint John River, water flows properly for half the day—over the falls into the Bay of Fundy. Then the spectacular tides of the bay come in. Pushed back by the incoming tide,the water reverses itself and proceeds to run uphill back over the falls and into the river again.

The famous Fundy tides cause other backward phenomena on the New Brunswick coast, too. Up the coast at Moncton, the "tidal bore" provides a two-a-day show. As regular as the rising and setting of the moon that pulls it, the high tide sweeps up the Petitcodiac River on a strict schedule. The wall of water rushes upriver—against the natural current to the sea—and the river flows backward until the tides go out again.

New Brunswick's other popular "backward" spot is the Magnetic Hill, near Moncton—a remarkably convincing optical illusion, rather than a natural phenomenon. Each year, thousands of baffled tourists drive *down* the small hill to a marked spot, turn off their engines, and watch open-mouthed as the car rolls slowly back *up* the hill.

Even New Brunswick's origins are slightly offbeat. The province was the last of the Atlantic Provinces to be settled, for it is the most rugged and forbidding. And its early settlers were some 28,000 United Empire Loyalists—the so-called "Tories" who fled the rebellious American colonies rather than fight the king to whom they were loyal. Most of the fleeing Tories were city-bred, from prominent Boston and New York families. They settled and struggled in the rugged New Brunswick wilderness. Fredericton, their capital, is one of Canada's most beautiful old cities. In the 1880's it was the source of the nation's first literary movement.

The coasts to which these first settlers came are frosted with sandy beaches and islands. But the northern uplands of New Brunswick are thickly forested and thinly settled—like the northern reaches of the Maine woods, which they border. Here, though, lies New Brunswick's real wealth—not only the pulp and paper from timber, but rich mineral and petroleum deposits that promise New Brunswick a prosperous future.

MONTREAL: ENTERTAINMENT FOR EVERYONE

THE "Paris of America" offers the arts a stimulating home and enthusiastic audiences. At this open-air symphony concert in Dominion Square, listeners are treated to both fine music and a splendid view of the city. Throughout the summer the "Theater under the Trees" in Lafontaine Park is attended by young and old people who enjoy jazz, folk, and band music.

The Montreal Symphony Orchestra, les Grand Ballets Canadians, and the Montreal Museum of Fine Arts have established the city as a center of the best in the artistic world. A new concert hall, acclaimed as one of the acoustically best in the world, has been completed as part of the "Place des Arts" cultural complex. Dozens of French-language theaters are found in the city; an International Film Festival is held annually.

To the Frenchman—and the gourmet of any nationality—*la cuisine* is another of the fine arts. Montreal is well known for its outstanding eating places. Though there are several private gourmet clubs, the city itself is almost a public gourmet club, with more than 4000 restaurants serving the foods of nearly every nation.

The city's businesses and stores are centered at Place Ville Marie in the cross-shaped skyscraper that towers over the new plaza. Beneath the building are more than fifty stores and boutiques where a customer can shop for elegant items without once going outside.

Visitors are greeted with hospitality in Montreal's large choice of restaurants.

No wonder the city has more than 11,000 hotels! Both residents and visitors have discovered that Montreal is truly the entertainment capital of Canada.

30

BAKING BREAD:
WORKING FAMILIES

BREAD and boats—symbols of the old-fashioned family and the rugged life of the fisherman—are sold on the farms and in the villages of Quebec's Gaspé Peninsula. On this tongue of land that juts out into the Gulf of St. Lawrence, life is quite different from that found in the more industrialized areas of Canada, though there are active copper mines here. Many people live in Gaspé, but the thickly forested, hilly land isolates them from each other, bringing quietness and a slow pace of living.

Our first view of the Gaspé makes it clear that its farmers and fishermen are predominantly French-Canadian. There is, everywhere, the air of provincial France. Many families are large and, characteristically, very close-knit. They work together, and there is work for every member of the family. The women and girls perform household duties and a few still use outdoor ovens to bake the warm, fragrant bread that is sold at the roadsides. The men and boys, when the farm work is done and the waters have frozen so that there is no more fishing, patiently create small, hand-carved wooden boats.

The Gaspé is ruggedly picturesque. Jagged, barren cliffs tower over the waters of the St. Lawrence, the Baie des Chaleurs, and the Atlantic, which surround the peninsula on three sides. In the Shickshocks Mountains, a national park has been established to provide shelter for such near-extinct animals as the wood caribou. Many tourists come to enjoy the excellent hunting and fishing, but the quietness remains dominant, and the feeling of Gaspé is a feeling of "family."

Life is simple in the Gaspé. Here, where the work is done in an enclosure of tree-laden greenness, there is an air of peace.

PERCÉ ROCK: CHANGING SILHOUETTE

IN the glowing red sky of sunrise, Percé Rock stands out sharp and black, its single wave-carved arch in sharp silhouette. For artists, photographers, and tourists who delight in its varying beauty, Percé has literally hundreds of faces. Geologically, it is simple—a broken-off promontory extending from the mainland of the Gaspé Peninsula. Waves have carved one arch in the pointed, shiplike rock, and it is slowly enlarging over the years.

In the morning light, Percé turns cool and gray. In the orange of sunset, it catches the colors and reflects them. From some angles it is like a great battleship, from others it appears incredibly delicate. At bright high noon its shadow is gone and it looks as quiet as "a painted ship upon a painted ocean." In other lights it seems to move gently on the bright blue water of the Gulf of St. Lawrence.

The ever-changing rock draws tourists to the bluffs that tower over the little village of Percé, named for its famous landmark. A little off the beaten path, and reached only by the one highway that encircles the peninsula, the village keeps its quiet charm. Artists mingle with French-Canadian fishermen; tourists come for a quick look and stay a week, caught in the spell of this far tip of the Gaspé.

At low tide, adventurous travelers may cross to Percé on a long sandbar. But more take the cruiser that circles the pierced (*percé*) rock, seeing still more of its continuously changing faces. The arch itself seems narrow from one angle, and like a huge natural bridge from another.

The boat speeds away and circles nearby Bonaventure Island, a sanctuary for thousands of white sea birds. It, too, was once a part of the peninsula, but has been separated from it by thousands of years of wave erosion. Here is another treat for artists and photographers—many rare birds are protected here, including the largest known colony of gannets, called here *Fous de Bassan*. What seems to be white patches of the rocky cliffs of the island is, we see at closer look, a dense gathering of feathery wings.

NOTRE DAME CHURCH: PIOUS SPLENDOR

THE breathtaking Church of Notre Dame is Montreal's "Mother Church." Visited by more than 150,000 tourists a year, it remains a revered place of worship for the city's thousands of Roman Catholics.

The present church on the Place d'Armes is the fifth Montreal church to carry the name. The original Notre Dame was a log chapel, built in 1642 by Sulpician priests in the tiny frontier settlement. The Sulpician Order still operates the church.

Completed in 1829, the Gothic-arched church is made of Montreal limestone. It is dominated by two square bell towers.

Inside, the church is a harmony of color. Its nearly 5000 pews are placed on a raised floor, giving everyone a clear view of the gilded altar. Stained-glass windows let in cascades of sparkling light. Near the main altar, built in 1878, is one of the largest organs in America.

Notre Dame is more than a beautiful showplace; it is still a parish church. Some worshippers still follow the Sulpician tradition of placing a tiny ship beneath a statue of the Virgin Mary for good luck before taking a voyage by sea.

Religion is an integral part of the history of French Canada. Another site of religious beauty is St. Joseph's Oratory, known as a place of miraculous healings. Crutches left by the grateful hang on the walls of this impressive shrine, which was built by the donations collected by one man, Brother Andre, a doorman at the Church of Notre Dame. Many visitors still make their pilgrimage by climbing the ninety-nine steps to the church on their knees.

St. Joseph's Oratory, built by the devotion of a single man.

WINTER CARNIVAL: A SNOWY PLAYGROUND

QUEBEC'S Winter Carnival turns the cold city into a Mardi Gras of ice sculpture, fireworks, street dancing, and floats. Here we look down on the dancing at the Grand Regency Ball, highlight of the carnival.

The Quebecois, tired of winter's restrictions, began the carnival in 1894. During the carnival, boredom is unknown. Quebec is a vigorous winter wonderland, with the accent on sports.

All sports-minded Canadians watch the Bonspiel Tournament, in which the nation's top curling teams compete. Skiers and sleighers glide down the slopes near the city's majestic Château Frontenac, center of indoor parties and gatherings. The entire countryside around this historic walled city joins in the fun.

Perhaps the most exciting event at the carnival is the ice-canoe race across the St. Lawrence River. Ice floes fill the river, and the paddlers use special canoes with steel or aluminum bands that cover the keel from bow to stern. These bands act like runners, allowing the crew to "drive" their canoe up and over the edge of an ice floe. Then, the canoers jump out, drag the boat across the ice to the next patch of water, shove it into the water and leap in even before it finishes splashing. Then they paddle to the next floe and begin the process again. It is a daring, cold, grueling sport. Professional crews, who come from the cities, used to find themselves losing to the country teams who learned, by necessity, to become experts in this dangerous method of transportation.

Each night, as fireworks glitter in the sky, the harshness of winter is forgotten. When the carnival is over, Quebec goes back to work.

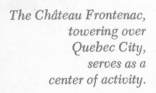

The Château Frontenac, towering over Quebec City, serves as a center of activity.

OTTAWA: THE NATION'S CAPITAL

HIGH over the spired rooftops of Ottawa fly hundreds of red and white flags, each with a single red maple leaf in the center, reminding one that the grandeur that is Ottawa is a working grandeur in which the complicated affairs of government are resolved.

On Parliament Hill, stately Gothic-arched buildings surrounded by huge lawns give Canada's capital a hushed, dignified appearance. Yet flowers, parks, and trees make the city gloriously colorful, especially during the annual Tulip Festival and the parading of Her Majesty's Royal Guards on Parliament Hill each summer morning.

Ottawa stands at the junction of three rivers: the Gatineau, the Rideau, and the Ottawa. Set on green-forested cliffs that rise from a quiet bay, the city represents a Canada that is proud, composed, and traditionally ceremonious.

Since she is Canada's head of state as well as Britain's, the Queen is never considered a visitor. When she is in Canada, she is "in residence." At such times, pageantry and festivities transform the city into a montage of royal splendor, as cheering crowds and the sound of music seem to echo from tower to tower.

Housed in the granite buildings are the two chambers of Canada's legislature, a Senate whose members are appointed for life, and a House of Commons, whose members are elected and serve until the end of Parliament. Their terms can be no longer than five years.

Formal power lies in the hands of the Governor General, who represents the Queen, and except on rare occasions acts solely on the advice of the Prime Minister and Cabinet. His chief duties are to open and close the sessions of Parliament and to give royal consent and so make law all bills passed by the Canadian Parliament.

Queen Elizabeth presents the colors to the regiments in front of Parliament Hill.

41

SCHOOLS:
KEEPING PACE
WITH THE WORLD

EDUCATION in Canada is progressing rapidly, keeping pace with the country's progress. More and more young people are going on to higher levels of education, as Canadians become aware that in the modern, technical, highly sophisticated world in which they live, trained and educated young men and women will be vitally needed.

Canada's schools are operated separately by each province. In Quebec and Newfoundland, education is denominational. The churches own and build their own schools, with the help of state funds.

The Yukon and Northwest Territories face special problems in education. With their vast expanses of land still to be worked, northern Canadians are especially aware of the need for education. Young Indian and Eskimo children are brought to the nearest town where there is a school and are housed in hostels or dormitories far away from their isolated homes.

Canada's many universities, both French and English, are excellent. More Canadians are getting a college education than ever before. New schools and additions to older schools are constantly being planned. Past this entranceway to Montreal's McGill University are modern buildings and facilities. French-speaking collegians in the city attend the massive University of Montreal, set high on a bluff.

Several provinces have established adult-education departments, with classes held in colleges, outdoors, or in homes. Here, adults who worked

Many modern schoolhouses are surrounded by mountain wilderness.

to open the new land are learning the modern methods needed to improve Canada and are keeping up with current world affairs. Small discussion groups spring up everywhere, for Canadians are aware that they are their country's future.

TORONTO: THE METROPOLITAN MYSTIQUE

TORONTO is a sophisticated modern metropolis. Canada's second-largest city, it is the headquarters of many businesses and industries. It is an important seaport and cultural center. Here is the city of big business, the city where money-making decisions are made, the "big city" to which dream-filled immigrants flock to seek their fortunes. The Toronto stock market is second only to New York on this continent in its volume of business.

Yet, Toronto is also one of the most "Canadian" of all Canada's cities. To many of its citizens, Toronto *is* Canada. Toronto is the cultural capital of English-speaking Canada. The production headquarters of the two television networks and all the major book publishers are located here, as is Canada's greatest university.

Toronto is a city with big-business know-how, excellent schools, and a new city hall that looks like two curved, glittering crystals. But it is equally a city of closely built red-brick houses, in which live people who have retained a homey, close-knit bond uncommon to most big cities. It has been called the most law-abiding, community-minded, and livable of all North American cities.

From Toronto Harbor oceangoing steamers and pleasure craft may view the city.

SHIPBUILDING:
CANADIAN
HERITAGE

THE Eskimos and Indians, Canada's earliest settlers, are thought to have come to this continent by walking over the frozen Bering Strait. But other explorers and settlers came to Canada by boat. Leif Ericson, a Norseman, may have landed on the Canadian shores as early as 1000 A.D. John Cabot came in 1497 and, after him, fishermen from Europe. Jacques Cartier, sailing from France, laid claim to Canada on ground touched by the St. Lawrence, and Samuel de Champlain founded the first colony on the river. Ships are so much a part of Canada's past and present that they cannot be overlooked.

Canada's earliest exploration was by water, not by land. Louis Jolliet and Father Jacques Marquette began their journey down the Mississippi from Canada in 1673. Sieur de La Salle followed them five years later, and journeyed over many of Canada's rivers.

The British could not have conquered Canada had it not been for their superior navy and the fact that most important French colonies and settlements were located on waterways.

Canada's West was tamed by her waterways. Covered wagons brought the people, but boats led the way. Hudson's Bay and other fur companies sailed their canoes into the western wilderness and filled them with animal skins. Wherever they went, they set up forts, some of which served as stopping grounds for overland travelers, and later became great cities.

The North, too, was first explored by water. Until the air age, sailing up the countless lakes and rivers was the only way to reach the Northwest Territories, the Yukon, and all areas north. In the winter, when the waters froze, the land was isolated.

Today, ocean steamers and freighters take to and from Canada goods that provide the largest share of her economy. And Canadian fishermen go out in their boats to reap the harvest of fish that keeps them alive.

Shipbuilding is no longer a big industry in Canada. Wooden ships, like the one being constructed here in Shelburne, Nova Scotia, are rare. Today's fishermen—even the Eskimos—use motorboats, many of which are made in Canada. They are a sign of progress that could not have been attained if explorers hundreds of years ago had not sailed their boats bravely into the unknown that was Canada.

UKRAINIAN DANCERS: PRIDE IN A HERITAGE

CANADA is a nation of many nationalities—not just the French and English we tend to think of. These Ukrainian folk dancers, dressed elaborately in their native costumes, are an example of the many groups who maintain the traditions of other lands. About a quarter of the Canadian population came originally from European countries other than France and England. Only about six per cent of the population were actually born in the British Isles. There are German, Czechoslovakian, Polish, Italian, Greek, Dutch, and Hungarian Canadians. The Scandinavian countries have also supplied Canada with many new citizens, as have Iceland, Japan, and China.

Many "new" Canadians have come from countries where they endured oppression or suffering. They came to Canada to worship in the way they chose and to live their lives in freedom. Immigrants have settled in all the provinces, both in the cities and the country, and they have become a vital part of Canadian life.

The new Canadians remain proud of their past and preserve the heritage of their homelands in many ways. At music festivals, held throughout the country, ornate native costumes are often worn. The people gather together to sing the songs and dance the dances of the lands they left. Various national groups participate in these festivals and learn to understand each other.

Most importantly, though, they are now Canadians. Every group can point to areas of community life in which they have excelled and where they have helped to improve their new home. Canada is not a melting pot where people lose their identity; she is a mosaic whose peoples are proud of their past identities, yet work together for the country they now share.

A Chinese public school in Victoria is a reminder of the lands across the Pacific.

49

SHAKESPEAREAN FESTIVAL

THE theater is dark as King Richard II speaks his lines, and the audience is transported back to a time in history filled with romance and courtliness:

I give this heavy weight from off my head
And this unwieldy sceptre from my hand,
The pride of kingly sway from out my heart;
With mine own tears I wash away my balm,
With mine own hands I give away my crown . . . .

Now, at the theater in Stratford, Ontario, the scenes come alive as notable casts perform the plays of William Shakespeare.

The sets allow little or no scenery, and the theater is a little bit like The Globe where Shakespeare originally presented his plays. Beautiful lawns surround the theater and white swans swim in the Avon.

The famous Shakespeare Festival, the most popular and most successful in North America, was begun at Stratford in 1953. Then, performances were held in a gigantic tent. But the ability of the performers and the excellent material with which they worked soon made Stratford successful enough to build the concrete and glass auditorium which seats 2000 people. Inside, the theater is somewhat Elizabethan in style, with seats curving in a steep crescent around the seven-level stage.

From June to October, Stratford buzzes with opera, jazz, and other forms of musical and theatrical events. But the highlight is the Shakespearean Company.

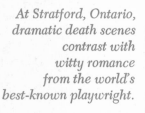

At Stratford, Ontario, dramatic death scenes contrast with witty romance from the world's best-known playwright.

"Mount, mount, my soul! thy seat is up on high; Whilst my gross flesh sinks downward, here to die."

So speaks Richard, as the play nears its end. With the bearing away of the casket containing the dead king and the remorse and repentance of his enemies, the curtain goes down. Once again, Shakespeare has lived on a stage much like his own.

HARVESTING WHEAT: GOLD IN THE PLAINS

SASKATCHEWAN'S Qu'Appelle Valley is the heart of Canada's breadbasket. Her endless miles of golden wheat prompted author Stephen Leacock to write, "The Lord said, 'Let there be wheat' and Saskatchewan was born."

Running like a giant furrow across almost the entire width of the province, the Qu'Appelle Valley is also a beautiful vacationland of streams, rivers, and lakes. The valley contains many landmarks of the opening of the West. Through it flows the Qu'Appelle River, which means the "river that calls." It called many people—settlers, fur trappers, hunters. The long stretches of cattle country in the southwest give the area the name "Great Lone Land."

Although wheat is the sturdy mainstay of the province, sportsmen know Saskatchewan better as a land of lakes and forests. In the largely unexplored north there are trout and pike, deer, duck, and geese.

A summer of warm days and cool nights brings visitors to Saskatchewan. But in the winter, the cold makes the land seem large, empty, and barren. Yet, Saskatchewan is a modern, progressive province. Regina, the capital, is an impressive city that bursts out of the flatlands. The completion of a dam on the South Saskatchewan River has given the province more than 500 miles of new shoreline for recreational facilities along a man-made 140-mile-long lake. The dam will make possible the irrigation and use of thousands of acres of plainsland, and the already vast wheat fields of Saskatchewan will continue to grow.

Mounties demonstrate horsemanship and other skills learned in Regina.

BANFF NATIONAL PARK

THE beauties of Banff National Park, largest of all Canadian playgrounds with its 2500 square miles, are at first almost overwhelming. There are fields of ice bordered by valleys that look like ribbons of green velvet. There are brilliant blue lakes crisscrossed with beavers' intricate dams. There are towering, ice-rimmed mountains where the most delicate of flowers grow haphazardly under your feet. There are resorts, hotels, monuments, schools, golf courses, horse and hiking trails, campgrounds, restaurants, and other recreational facilities made by man.

Mount Assiniboine, the "Matterhorn of the Rockies," rising 11,870 feet, can be viewed from cabins set far apart in the valleys or along the trails that climb steeply up over mountains. The town of Banff is surrounded by grand sweeps of mountains, giving visitors a feeling of being away from the rest of the world while enjoying its comforts.

Canadians recognized the rare beauty of the eastern slopes of the Rocky Mountains in Alberta as early as 1885, when Banff became the country's first designated national park. And it would be difficult to leave Banff except for the cheering knowledge that throughout Canada,

Solitude and beauty on a canoe ride on Banff's Lake Louise.

in all the provinces, there are other national and provincial parks. Some have mountains, some lakes, some forests, some spots of historical interest. All of them were created in the belief that man needs clean fresh air and space to roam, explore, and be alone. In the natural wilderness of her parks, Canada has given man these gifts.

LOGGERS: RIDING TO THE SAWMILL

TODAY, modern tractors, trucks, and snowmobiles haul lumber from the thirty-seven per cent of Canada's land which is forested. In the old days, however, sheer skill, muscle, and nerve were used to get the lumber to the sawmills.

In the early years of the settlement of North America, forests were cut down to make room for farms and towns. Sawmills were erected by the entire community. It was not until the early 1900's that logging became a special trade for rugged men who risked their lives to cut down the thousands of acres of lumber that lay "beyond the East."

Loggers of those days were propertyless men who lived in wretched, crowded, one-room buildings as they cut their way across the country. At every moment, their lives were in danger. They could be killed by falling timber, crushed on a log landing, or most feared of all, meet their deaths in a jam, when the logs on their way down the river stuck and piled on top of each other until there was a high wall of wood heaving gently back and forth. To break a jam, the "king log" had to be found. This was the log which, when moved, would free the backup and send the logs leaping on their journey with a swift jerk. Many men unable to get off the jam in time were killed. Such unfortunate men were the subjects of many of the songs sung by the loggers.

Dressed in their red flannel shirts and long boots, the loggers worked fourteen-hour days. Their lives were rough and lonely, and they yearned for the day when they could go to town.

Every year, the loggers from many camps would gather together for a log birling contest. Two men would board a log floating in the river, one on each end, and turning the log with their feet, try to dislodge each other. When all but two participants had been eliminated, the final contest between experts would often last a full day.

Today, the logger's life is much easier. Electricity, better housing, and excellent food are his lot. Yet life in the forests of giant trees still requires a special breed of brave, rugged men.

SPORTS:
A WAY OF LIFE
IN CANADA

CANADIAN sportsmen are both enthusiastic viewers and dedicated participants. Cheering is equally spirited at professional hockey games and at Pee Wee Games in small towns, like the game pictured here.

Even small children participate in the numerous leagues found in every province. Little boys just learning to skate move determinedly over the ice, dreaming of the day when they will wear a Toronto Maple Leaf or Montreal Canadien uniform and bring glory to their town. Sometimes, they even dare dream of scoring the goal that wins the coveted Stanley Cup.

Basically, hockey is a simple game. Each team tries to knock the puck (a round, frozen piece of rubber) into a net which is guarded by a "goalie," a player who must have quick reflexes and real courage, since the puck can reach speeds of over 100 miles an hour. Besides the goalie, each team has five men on the ice: three forwards, whose job it is to place the puck in the opponents' net, and two defense men, who try to keep the opponent from scoring. Watching the incredibly fast action and the smooth cooperation of the players, it is easy to forget that these feats are being performed on skates.

Many other sports are popular with the vigorous Canadians, who use their natural resources—lakes, forests, wilderness, mountains, rivers—winter and summer.

Scottish regiments quartered in Quebec introduced Canadians to the sport of curling in 1768. Today, curling rinks are found everywhere. Often wearing colorful tam-o'-shanters, the curlers slide stones across an alley of ice toward a circular painted target 130 feet away. Teammates with brooms "sweep" the path of the oncoming stone, skillfully guiding its course and speed. Points are given for the closeness of the stones to the target. Less rugged than hockey, curling demands quick thinking, exact moves, and concentration.

MANITOBA'S LAKES: HISTORIC BEGINNING

IF there had been no Ice Age, fish such as this could not be caught in Manitoba. For in pre-glacial times, the lowland of the province was the basin of an enormous lake. As the glaciers melted, they dumped boulders, earth, and pebbles, filling up the lake bed and leaving an irregular surface of hollows that became smaller lakes. Manitoba's main lakes—Winnipeg, Winnipegosis, Manitoba, Cedar, and Moose—are just "puddles" left by that huge mass of water, called Lake Agassiz in honor of the Swiss geologist, Louis Agassiz, who proved the extent of the Ice Age in North America. Today, Manitoba fishermen and vacationers relax at the province's thousands of lakes.

All of Canada was once covered with glacial ice, in some places a mile thick. The pressure was so great on the land that the surface of the earth pushed down as much as 1000 feet.

Much of Canada's spectacular scenery owes a direct debt to the glaciers. They formed in the far north, as for many years more snow fell yearly than was melted. Temperatures, then, of course, were extremely low, and summers short. The Ice Age is believed to have ended because of a change in climate in Canada. The summers became longer and hotter and less ice survived the increased heat. Glaciers, of course, have by no means disappeared. Canada herself has many small ones—valley glaciers and ice fields in the Canadian Rockies and ice caps in the Arctic. Furthermore, some scientists say that should the average yearly temperature of this region fall ten degrees, another Ice Age could begin!

Her thousands of lakes help make Manitoba a busy resort area.

SILENCED CANNON: REMNANT OF THE PAST

ON unmoving wheels, cannon like this one look out over the same Red River made famous by song. They stand silently at Fort Garry, Manitoba, a bastioned stone fort used in the early 1800's by the Hudson's Bay Company as its post for northern fur trade with the Indians. Today, the fort is part of a National Historic Park located just outside the modern city of Winnipeg.

Before the West was tamed, Fort Garry was the starting point of many a pioneer's journey through the wilderness to a new home. Over the river came boats filled with animal skins. Wagons called Red River Carts floated across the river bearing pioneers to one of the last points of civilization. Their wagons loaded, families would sit around campfires on the riverbank and say good-bye to their friends and to the security the fort provided them. As we stand behind the cannon, looking out on the quietness of what was once a bustling, crowded river, we can almost hear them:

> Come and sit by my side if you love me.
> Do not hasten to bid me adieu.
> But remember the Red River Valley.
> And the boy who has loved you so true.

Many other reminders of the past still linger in the province of Manitoba. Fort Prince of Wales, near Churchill, was built in the 1770's by the British. The fort has walls forty-two feet thick, and took twenty years to build. Still, when the French attacked in 1782, the British defenders surrendered without a shot being fired—because the troops were out in the nearby woods hunting duck.

Canada's West is filled with many symbols of a rugged frontier past, constant reminders of the people who made Canada the modern, prosperous country she is today. But in Canada, the frontier is not just a picturesque memory. To the north, Canada's frontier still beckons and challenges these people who have already tamed so many thousands of miles of wilderness.

VICTORIA:
A SUMMER
OF FLOWERS

VICTORIA is a city in love with nature. Warmed by the Japanese Current, which keeps the weather temperate the year round, the city is alive with color. The blues of the Pacific surround green lawns, cool gray stone buildings and, everywhere, the riotous colors of flowers. In Victoria, even the lampposts are adorned with flowers.

As we look down on the capital of British Columbia, the city seems to be cradling its Inner Harbor, shared by ocean steamers and pleasure craft. Here two of the city's major sources of income, giant Douglas firs and fish from huge canneries, begin their journey across the Pacific.

Victoria is on Vancouver Island, southwest of the British Columbia mainland. It has become a tourist's favorite, for not only the weather but the scenery is ideal, having the air of an English country town set in the rugged beauty of western Canada. There are crisply clipped formal hedges, lawns dense with flowers, and lovely gardens, the most impressive being Beacon Hill Park, a 154-acre gardener's dream, and the beautiful Butchart Gardens. In Thunderbird Park, authentic totem poles represent the five Indian tribes that once inhabited all of British Columbia. Centennial Square, with its new city hall, and the formal grounds for the ornate provincial legislative buildings are havens of greenness.

The most English of all Canada's cities, Victoria exudes a calm, relaxed atmosphere where one can enjoy freshwater fishing and swimming or leisurely cups of tea in picturesque English restaurants. Beauty is everywhere to be enjoyed in Victoria, and it is a city that believes in taking the time to enjoy all of it.

Victoria's Inner Harbor, shared by ocean steamers and pleasure craft.

FLOWERS: A REMINDER OF THE WILDERNESS

IN British Columbia, these baskets of bright flowers hang from white-globed streetlights. In the Yukon, the women plant window boxes to relieve the whiteness of the snow. On Prince Edward Island and in Banff National Park, wild flowers grow densely and haphazardly. In Ottawa, Vancouver, Toronto, Quebec, Montreal—in great cities and small towns—well-cared-for flower gardens dot the parks and surround government buildings and monuments. Everywhere we go in Canada we see flowers—flowers left alone to grow naturally and flowers meticulously planted and nurtured.

They are an English heritage, these flowers, brought to Canada by those who fondly remembered country gardens. But Canada has made them her own.

The flowers are a symbol of a happy people who live in freedom and prosperity. Some Canadians live on farms and use modern machines to plant and harvest. Others live in big cities with skyscrapers and glass and efficient subways. Some fish from motorboats, or process fish on huge assembly lines. All of them have remained aware of the spaciousness and of the promise of their land which, no matter how much it has progressed, remains mostly wilderness.

Children learn early about the beauty of nature.

Canadians know that they share their great land with nature, that they have not earned all of it yet. Northward, Canada is yet to be claimed. Through the flowers, Canadians keep in touch with the nature that is so much a part of them and their nation and their future.

EXPORTING LUMBER: SHIPS TO MANY LANDS

THE lumber being loaded into this huge freighter may someday become the front page of the New York *Times* or the Toronto *Star*. Such huge ocean freighters are familiar sights throughout Canada. Riding low in the water, they leave ports on the Atlantic, Pacific, and St. Lawrence Seaway filled with newsprint, fish, and the products of mines.

About twenty-three per cent of the total land area of Canada is presently or potentially productive forest. About the same percentage is unproductive forest. Newsprint is the nation's biggest export. Her pulp and paper mills supply most of the big northern United States cities with their growing need for this product.

Salmon, lobster, cod, herring, and haddock are among the more important fish products sent abroad, with Vancouver, in the Pacific Northwest, supporting the biggest fish-canning industries. Wheat is the country's main farm export. Tons of this nutritious yellow grain are sent to nations that cannot grow enough food to feed their people.

Canada's role as a major exporter has heightened her interest and importance in world affairs. The ships that enter her many ports bring people and ideas as well as the products of other nations, and Canada has gained a respected voice in the making of world policies.

British General James Wolfe was a great admirer of the potential of Canada. "This will sometime hence be a vast empire," he wrote, "the seat of power and learning. Nature has refused them nothing, and there will grow a people . . . that will fill this vast space."

Giant grain elevators stand behind the workers who ready logs to be made into pulpwood.

69

INDIAN
TOTEM POLE:
CARRYING ON
A HERITAGE

CANADA'S diversity of peoples and heritages has given her a rich storehouse of native skills and crafts. Ancient folk arts—the tribal skills of Eskimos and Indians—produce marvels like this huge totem pole being carved for England's (and Canada's) queen. And the traditional skills of the French, British, and other European groups produce many interesting and beautiful items.

The arts of the Eskimo and the Indian—some decorative, some based on religion and magic—have passed from generation to generation for hundreds of years. Only recently has the outside world "discovered" the subtle Eskimo art forms—simply sophisticated block prints and small sculptures, carved from soapstone. Eskimo women make charming toys from sealskin; once made just for the children of the tribe, they are now widely sold.

The Indians of the Pacific Northwest are best known for their symbolic tribal totem poles. The carving—and the accompanying tracing of history and ancestry—is fast becoming a lost art among modern Indians. It is preserved in places such as Thunderbird Park in Victoria, B.C. Indians throughout Canada still fashion the traditional decorative pottery, sealskin moccasins, and copper and silver jewelry.

A long tradition of cloth-making was part of the heritage of settlers from both England and France. The necessities of "do-it-yourself" frontier life kept this art alive, and even now, throughout the eastern provinces, we can discover finely woven wool blankets and skirts, beautiful tweeds and wools, handsome sweaters. Ile d'Orleans, the pastoral French island in the St. Lawrence River near Quebec, is home for many fine weavers. Enterprises range from tiny one-woman handlooms to great weaving mills.

Similarly, the wood-carving tradition was brought to Canada from Europe. Tiny handmade boats, figures, and plaques can be seen throughout French Canada.

Schools to protect, preserve, and encourage handicrafts are becoming increasingly popular in Canada.

THE ESKIMO:
LOVE OF
A WAY OF LIFE

FOLLOWING a way of life that has changed little in thousands of years, this Eskimo family is setting up a camp. It is summer, and the family is moving from an ice igloo into a canvas tent igloo. (In the Eskimo language, any form of home is called an "igloo".)

Most of Canada's Eskimos live in the Northwest Territories. Groups of related families wander throughout a vaguely defined area, fishing, hunting, and trapping. Dogsleds are still used for land travel, but in the waters, outboard motorboats are rapidly replacing the kayak.

The Eskimo's life is a cold, resourceful struggle for the barest necessities. From the animals he hunts—caribou, seals, whales—he takes the meat for food, uses the fat for light, the sinews for thread, and the hide for clothes, bedding, and footwear. But more and more we notice traces of the modern world. Many igloos today have small stoves. The hunters and fishermen sell or exchange what is left of the catch to government-backed cooperative stores. Here, too, are sold the finely detailed Eskimo artwork and sculpture, currently prized by art galleries throughout North America.

Traditional resources are no longer to be found in quantities great enough to support the Eskimos. Many of them are moving into the towns. There they work for such government projects as commercial fisheries and at DEW (Distant Early Warning) Line observation posts. The government, aware of the plight of the Eskimo, has established many schools for vocational training of both young and old.

In the towns, the Eskimos live in modern wooden houses and enjoy such luxuries as coffeepots, blankets, and radios. About seventy-five per cent of all Eskimo children go to school, where they learn about the vast technical world that lies to the South. Yet, many of them return to the wilderness, harboring a love of the simple, hard-working life of fishing and hunting in "Nunassiaq," the Good Land.

HUDSON'S BAY COMPANY

IN 1670, the major power in Canada was neither France nor England, but the Hudson's Bay Company, which controlled one-third of the territory of Canada. Over a million square acres of land were given to them to govern for the purpose of bartering with the Indians and exporting furs and skins to England. Very little was required of the company in return for so vast a bequest. One stipulation was that whenever a member of the English royal family entered the territory, he was to be given two elks and two black beavers!

For nearly 200 years, "The Governor and Company of Adventurers of England Trading into Hudson's Bay," as the company was called officially, wielded great power and filled their journals with stories of adventure in the North and West frontiers.

The company's traders were mostly nomadic, building many forts but no actual settlements. They lived lives of solitude, and grew fiercely loyal to their employer. Over and over, the company produced heroes like Samuel Hearne, who at the age of twenty-four set out to discover a Northwest Passage and the copper mines which the Indians claimed lay to the north. Twice he set out unsuccessfully, but he could not be persuaded to give up his search. He set out again in December, 1770, making a map of the Hudson Bay area that was to serve men for the following hundred years. Hearne and his companions crossed the Arctic Circle, and though they found few copper mines, they returned with a vast knowledge of the area never before known.

Today, the Hudson's Bay Company's traders live a less rugged life. Eskimos and Indians still carry their catch to the red-trimmed white buildings at well over a hundred trading posts. But the company itself has vastly expanded. With headquarters in Winnipeg, the Hudson's Bay Company operates many supermarkets and modern department stores in some of Canada's larger cities. They have made an import agreement with the United States and own great quantities of mineral rights in Canada's rich West. Their name remains a proud one, for had it not been for the bravery and discoveries of the early fur traders who claimed the land, Canada may not have been a nation today.

PANNING
FOR GOLD:
HIGH HOPES
IN THE YUKON

GOLD!" was the cry that first brought prospectors to Canada's far, frozen North. For the Yukon Territory, like the rest of Canada, is blessed with nature's riches—gold, silver, lead, zinc, and oil deposits that are only beginning to be tapped. The vast, cold land stretches to the edge of the Arctic Circle, a land where men can explore and, if they are lucky, catch sight of white polar bears blending with the ice floes on which they silently glide.

The Yukon became famous in 1896 when George Carmack, a prospector, scooped gold out of a stream he named "Bonanza." More than 40,000 people rushed to the area. Soon Dawson City, once a small settlement, was filled with dance halls, hotels, and saloons, and the Yukon became a raucous, exciting land. When the Gold Rush ended, Dawson became a ghost town, and the Yukon slipped back to its quiet ways. Prospectors still searched for gold and fur traders trekked through the wilderness. Then the Yukon was opened up again as the 1523-mile Alaska Highway was built from Dawson Creek, British Columbia, to Fairbanks, Alaska. When the highway was completed in 1942, the Yukon again began to grow.

Whitehorse, the capital, is today a city of white buildings, modern hotels, and paved sidewalks. The annual Sourdough Rendezvous, when Yukoners celebrate the passing of another dark winter and look forward to the sunshine and profusion of flowers coming with the spring, is a colorful and exciting three-day carnival.

Stern-wheelers on the banks of the Yukon River at Whitehorse are symbols of a wild and glorious past.

EXPO '67:
SPECTACLE
OF THE
CENTURY

HOUSES stacked Pueblo-Indian style, with one man's roof forming another man's garden, space capsules scorched in actual flight, monorail trains, food from scores of nations, world art treasures, and the finest entertainment in the cultural world were features of Expo '67, Canada's Universal and International Exposition.

"Habitat '67" was one of the main attractions of the fair. The seemingly jumbled, but brilliantly planned, housing project was one of the exhibits left standing when the exhibition ended. It is an example of the lasting benefits that can come from a world's fair. Many people were able to view for the first time examples of art, both in pictures and in music, and all who came gained a better understanding of the habits and thoughts of other people.

The fair was built on islands in the St. Lawrence River, opposite the Montreal harbor. One of the islands is natural, two are man-made. Seen at night from the mainland of Montreal, with fireworks reflected in the water, the islands looked like a twinkling dreamland. The buildings of more than seventy nations were toured by hundreds of thousands of visitors—exceeding all expectations—who covered the immense site on foot and in boats, trains, rickshaws, and buses.

The theme of Expo was "Man and His World," and exhibitions proudly proclaiming man's role in society, in sciences, in medicine, and in the arts were done so creatively that the fair as a whole was an example of man's ingenuity. Educational and entertaining, Expo was an experience not soon forgotten.

Expo '67 took place during Canada's centennial year, when the whole nation was celebrating. Yet, Expo was the high point of the festival, and a fitting tribute to the advancements the nation has made in a century of existence. "Come to Canada!" was the call to Expo, and those who came visited not only the fair but areas en route, taking home with them impressions that will benefit Canada's tourist, industrial, and commercial trades for years to come.

SOME IMPORTANT DATES IN CANADIAN HISTORY

1000	*Leif Ericson, Norseman, led an expedition from Greenland to the shores of what was probably Canada.*
1497	*John Cabot, sailing from Bristol, England, reached the shores of Canada.*
1534	*An expedition, led by Jacques Cartier, entered the Gulf of St. Lawrence and sailed up the river to where Montreal now stands.*
1604	*First permanent French colony in North America, Port Royal, founded by Samuel de Champlain.*
1608	*Settlement of Quebec begun by Champlain at the site of the narrowing of the St. Lawrence estuary.*
1629	*Champlain forced to surrender Quebec to the English when a small British fleet appeared at the St. Lawrence.*
1632	*Canada restored to France by the Treaty of St. Germain-en-Laye.*
1659	*Pierre Radisson and Medart Chouart, making use of the inter-connected lake and river system, penetrated beyond the Great Lakes and were probably the first Europeans to see the Upper Mississippi.*
1663	*New France became a Royal Province modeled on French provinces.*
1665	*French mission established on the shores of Lake Superior.*
1673	*Jolliet and Marquette reach and descend the Mississippi.*
1682	*LaSalle took possession of the valley of the Mississippi down to the Gulf of Mexico in the name of Louis XIV, calling it Louisiana.*
1713	*Under the Treaty of Utrecht, France yielded to Britain her claims to the Hudson Bay area, Newfoundland, and Nova Scotia.*
1759	*The capture of Quebec by the British.*
1763	*By the Peace of Paris Treaty, Canada was ceded to Great Britain.*
1774	*Establishment of the Province of Quebec, which includes Canada and all the western territory which France had claimed.*
1775-76	*American Revolutionaries tried unsuccessfully to capture Canada.*
1791	*Canada divided at the Ottawa River into two parts: Lower Canada, mostly French; and Upper Canada, British.*
1837	*Rebellions in Upper and Lower Canada.*
1840	*Canada reunited.*
1848	*Responsible government rule over its own internal affairs achieved in Canada and Nova Scotia.*
1854	*Reciprocity treaty with United States gave Canadian natural products free entrance to the United States market.*
1867	*Canada became the first federal union in the British Empire. Ontario, Quebec, Nova Scotia, and New Brunswick entered the union.*
1870	*Manitoba joined the Canadian Confederation.*
1871	*British Columbia joined the Canadian Confederation.*
1873	*Prince Edward Island joined the Canadian Confederation.*
1885	*Northwest Rebellion led by Louis Riel.*
1885	*Completion of the Canadian Pacific Railway linked East and West.*
1905	*Alberta and Saskatchewan joined the Canadian Confederation.*
1914	*Canada joined the Allies in World War I.*
1939	*Canada declared war on Germany during World War II.*
1947	*Newfoundland joined Canada, forming the current ten provinces.*
1955	*Construction begun on St. Lawrence Seaway linking United States and Canadian ports accessible to oceangoing vessels.*
1967	*Expo 67—World's Fair to celebrate Canada's hundredth birthday.*

SOME FAMOUS NAMES IN CANADIAN HISTORY

JOHN CABOT (1450-1498)—*English seaman who was the first man to reach the shores of Canada, reaching Newfoundland in 1497.*

JACQUES CARTIER (1491-1557)—*A seaman of St. Malo, France. In 1534 he led an expedition up the St. Lawrence River to the spot where Montreal now stands, claiming the land for France.*

SAMUEL DE CHAMPLAIN (1570-1635)—*Frenchman who, in the interest of fur trading, sailed up the St. Lawrence River and in 1604 helped found the first French colony in North America at Port Royal, Acadia. In 1608, he began the settlement of Quebec. Until his death, he remained in Canada, exploring the interior land and helping promote the fur trade.*

WILLIAM LYON MACKENZIE KING (1874-1950)—*Canadian statesman, prime minister of Canada 1921-30 and 1935-48. Completed Canada's independence from Britain in the field of foreign affairs. Kept English and French Canada united through World War II.*

SIR ALEXANDER MACKENZIE (1764-1820)—*Explorer who found the first overland trail to the Pacific, opening the way for traders.*

SIR JOHN ALEXANDER MACDONALD (1815-1891)—*First prime minister of Canada, serving from 1867 to 1873 and 1878 to 1891. Founder of a national policy in 1878 and responsible for the completion of the Canadian Pacific Railway in 1885.*

SIR WILFRED LAURIER (1841-1919)—*Leader of the Liberal party from 1887 to 1919, and prime minister from 1896 to 1911. A strong nationalist, he inaugurated the policy of a Canadian navy separate from Britain's.*

SIR WILLIAM OSLER (1849-1919)—*Physician and professor, McGill Medical School. More than anyone else, founder of modern medical practice. Author of* Principles and Practice of Medicine.

LOUIS RIEL (1844-1885)—*A French-Canadian nationalist, Riel seized control of Fort Garry in 1869 in an effort to guarantee the right of the French half-breeds in Manitoba to keep their lands and identities. Though he fled when a large military expedition appeared, he was the real founder of the province of Manitoba. In the spring of 1885, he set up a provisional government in the Saskatchewan valley, announcing separation from the Roman Catholic church, and denying the authority of Canada. A military force defeated the rebels, and Riel was taken prisoner and hanged late in that year.*

STEPHEN BUTLER LEACOCK (1869-1944)—*A professor of political economy, Leacock is best remembered for his satirical humor, such as* Sunshine Sketches of a Little Town.

LUCY MAUD MONTGOMERY (1877-1942)—*Author of* Anne of Green Gables, *her stories were set in the Prince Edward Island background into which she was born.*

MAZO DE LA ROCHE (1885-   )—*Novelist famous for a series of books about the Whiteoak family, set in Ontario.*

SIR FREDERICK GRANT BANTING (1891-1941)—*Discovered insulin as a remedy for diabetes in 1921, for which he was awarded the Nobel Prize for medicine.*

RIGHT HONOURABLE LESTER BOWLES PEARSON (1897-   )—*Nobel Peace Prize winner in 1957, prime minister of Canada from April, 1963 to April, 1968.*

SOME FRENCH-CANADIAN WORDS AND PHRASES

The following words and phrases would be useful for a visitor to the French-speaking areas of Canada.

Good-morning, good day.	Bonjour (*bohn*-ZHOOR)
Good-bye.	Au revoir (*oh*-VWAHR)
Good evening, good night.	Bonsoir (*bohn*-SWAHR)
How are you? How do you do?	Comment allez-vous? (*koh-mahn tah-lay* VOO)
Fine, thank you.	Bien, merci (BE-EN, *mare-see*)
I'm sorry.	Je regrette (*zhuh reh*-GRET)
Excuse me.	Excuze-moi (*ex-kew-zay*-MWAH)
Thank you very much.	Merci bien (MARE-*see be-en*)
Do you speak English?	Parlez-vous Anglais? (*par-lay*-VOO ZAHN-*glay*)
I don't understand.	Je ne comprends pas (*zhuh nuh* KOM-*prahn* PAH)
My name is . . .	Je m'appelle . . . (*zhuh* MAH-*pel*)
I would like you to meet . . .	Je vous présente (ZHUH *voo* PRAY-*zahnt*)
What time is it?	Quelle heure est-il? (*kel er ay*-TEEL)
What do you want?	Que voulez-vous? (KUH *voo-lay-voo*)
Where is it?	Où est-ce? (*oo* ESS)
Where are they?	Où sont-ils? (*oo sahn*-TEEL)
(Acknowledging an introduction)	Enchantée (*ahn-shahn*-TAY)

NUMBERS

One   Un (UHN)
Two   Deux (DUH)
Three   Trois (TRWAH)
Four   Quatre (KAH-*truh*)
Five   Cinq (SANK)
Six   Six (SEESS)
Seven   Sept (SEHT)
Eight   Huit (HWEET)
Nine   Neuf (NUHF)
Ten   Dix (DEESS)

DAYS OF THE WEEK

Sunday   Dimanche (*dee*-MAHNSH)
Monday   Lundi (LUHN-*dee*)
Tuesday   Mardi (MAR-*dee*)
Wednesday   Mercredi (MARE-*kruh-dee*)
Thursday   Jeudi (ZHUH-*dee*)
Friday   Vendredi (VAHN-*druh-dee*)
Saturday   Samedi (SAM-*dee*)

INDEX